MAJESTIC
JAIPUR

Text by Sara Wheeler
Photography by Tarun Chopra

Prakash Books

Half Title
*Maharaja Sawai Jai Singh II as painted
by Sahib Ram, AD 1740. Courtesy City
Palace Museum, Jaipur*

Title spread
*The best time to approach Amber is at
dawn when shafts of the early morning
sun illuminate the imposing ramparts of
the sprawling fortress*

Right
*When seen from a distance, Jal Mahal
gleams like a jewel set in the calm waters
of the Man Sagar Lake*

Pages 6-7
*A view of the city of Jaipur from
Nahargarh Fort*

Pages 8-9
*Local women draped in vibrant red
odhnis or veils add a splash of colour to
an elephant polo match at Chaugan
Stadium below Nahargarh Fort*

Pages 10-11
*Polo Jaipur style. A slower more sedate
version of the game where elephants
lumber across the field, steered by their
mahouts, while players try to manoeuvre
the ball with their sticks*

Pages 12-13
*Hanuman leaps across the ornate gates
leading into Diggi Palace*

Distributed in India by
Prakash Book Depot
M-86, Connaught Circus
New Delhi 110 001

Captions: Aruna Ghose
Editor: Aruna Ghose
Design: Gul;morhur Press, New Delhi

ISBN 962-217-457-4

Printed in Hong Kong

INTRODUCTION

The celebrated lipstick-pink crenellated walls, perforated with musket and cannon holes and embroidered with towers and parapets, look like a hardboard film set at first glance. This is Jaipur, coloured pink by the Rajputs to symbolise hospitality and, the oldest surviving urban centre in northern India to be built to a plan. Not a crumbling shell of another culture which rose and fell amidst the shifting sands of Indian history, it is a vibrant and burgeoning modern metropolis and the 12th largest city in the country. The old city is a constant and colourful mêlée, and if the way ahead is blocked, the hapless Jaipuri simply swerves across the road and proceeds on the wrong side. Bikes, rickshaws, autorickshaws and the ubiquitous Ambassadors and Marutis squeeze through the narrow gates while angular and milky-white cows moon across the lanes of traffic and pigs rooting among piles of rubbish compete for space with playful goats.

Yet even amidst this maelstrom it is still evident that Jaipur began life as a well-planned town on a neat urban grid. Even in the filthy road leading north from the Chandpol Gate where naked children wash themselves at the roadside pump, the old drainage channels are in place. The ranks of arched shop-fronts on the main street are part of a carefully-executed symmetrical design, and the royal buildings reveal the 18th-century synthesis of Mughal and Rajput architecture so characteristic of the magnificent city of Jaipur.

The city's main artery runs horizontally from Chandpol to Surajpol Gate. Until the 20th century the seven gates of Jaipur, linked by the famous pink wall and each with two kiosks above and machicolations over the entrance, were kept locked at night. Large sections of the wall, alas, have disappeared, probably for secondary use as building material; it is sad to record that a great deal of the heritage of Jaipur has been eroded either by greed or by need.

Jaipur is liberally splashed with colour. Mounds of gleaming scarlet chillies fringe the Chandpol Bazaar, at its western end a particularly seething and slow-moving mass of humanity, especially in the morning rush. Hundreds of fruit and vegetable sellers bunch around the old town's main circus, the Badi Chaupar. Women from outlying villages adjust canvas canopies or squat alongside their pyramids of strange-shaped fruit, bright of plumage in their ankle bracelets, toerings and bangles. Rosita Forbes, writing just before the Second World War, commented, 'the streets of Jaipur look as if all the Impressionists had upset their paintboxes'.

Climb to the Monkey Temple near Bari Chaupar for a fine view of Jaipur in action. A steady trickle of local inhabitants appear to sprinkle grain over the flat roof, food for the monkeys and good *karma* for the feeders, while women sit cross-legged in the temple listening to priests intone. Monkey smells and incense fragrance compete with the drifts of pungent spices from the lurid cones in the booths under the arched Tripolia Bazaar opposite. The road is wide (every

Sawai Man Singh II with Gayatri Devi, London, late 1930s

Coat of Arms at the entrance to Raj Mahal

15

Vignettes of street life in Jaipur. A local dentist with a patient; a tailor attaches a tinsel border to an odhni or veil

traveller to Jaipur, especially those who came in the 19th century, has commented on the pleasing and unusual width of the main streets), and while the pavements are pock-marked and cracked, the tarmac is surprisingly smooth in spite of the heavy flow of traffic through the city.

The Hawa Mahal, the signature building of Jaipur, is also very near Bari Chaupar. It was built of sandstone in 1799 by the architect Lalchand Usta for Pratap Singh, the maharaja who reigned from 1778 to 1803 and who was something of a poet and composer. The Hawa Mahal, Palace of the Winds, has a fanciful five-storey pyramidal façade of semi-octagonal overhanging windows with perforated screens; it is a baroque honeycombed fantasy one-room deep. One 19th-century traveller dismissed it as 'a mere mask of stucco', but Sir Edwin Arnold described it more poetically as 'a vision of daring and dainty loveliness'. This piece of artistic exuberance was, however, intended as a discreet vantage-point from which the ladies of the court, languishing in purdah, could watch the action in the street below through latticed windows.

The Johari Bazaar on the road down to the Sanganer Gate spills over with brightly coloured fabric markets and workshops where craftsmen fashion gold jewellery in the kundan-style, long associated with Jaipur and characterised by inlaid gems. Enamelling is still widely practiced, as it has been since Sikh practitioners were imported to the court as far back as the 16th century. Along with Partapgarh in southern Rajasthan, Jaipur is known for enamelwork in gold, mother of pearl and glass. There are three basic craft forms of which the third — incrustation — was described by Sir George Birdwood as 'the master art of the world'.

The warren of old city streets melts into the zigzag approach road to the Nahargarh (tiger) Fort at one end of the parched Kali Khoh ridge. Drying pats of buffalo dung, gathered for fuel, have replaced prowling tigers on the slopes, and at the lower edges a raisin-eyed woman arrives with fresh supplies, squinting into the sunlight as she wearily unloads her worn saddlebags.

Men at the entrance to the fort-palace are playing cricket with a yellow bat, and the hollow tap of ball against willow breaks the silence. The Kachchwaha dynasty captured the ancient fort, then known as Sudarshangarh, from the Mina tribe; it was rebuilt in 1734 by the ruler Jai Singh II and expanded in 1868 and again in 1902–3. The exterior walls have trompe l'oeil shutters and the inside of Nahargarh consists of a dilapidated maze of rooms, narrow corridors and courtyards spread over two levels; the royal family lived downstairs in the winter while in summer, they moved upstairs. The best rooms are tiled and latticed with jaliwork, like delicate marble filigree.

From this hilltop fort observe how the old city clusters around the spacious palace complex on the northern fringe of the urban grid. Entering the palace from the main street is like discovering an oasis in the centre of the bustle; it is the tranquility of this and the greenery of the many palace gardens that make Jaipur such a multi-faceted city. The palace, once the official residence of the maharaja, is not one building but a sequence of them separated by interconnecting courtyards and gardens. Gayatri Devi, the third wife of the last maharaja who came to the throne in 1922 aged just eleven, was carried in on a palanquin on her wedding day and she described it as 'almost a town in itself'. She had to sit still while the 400-odd women living in the zenana as well as the noblewomen of Jaipur filed passed her, parting her veil to get a good look and dropping a gift in her lap. If they didn't like the look of her, they said so.

The main entrance to the palace is through the Sire Deorhi Gate on the east side, and it leads into the Jaleb Chowk outer courtyard with the Naqqar Khana or Drum House to one side. Jai Singh founded the palace in the 18th century, but some parts were added later, for example the Mubarak Mahal (Palace of Welcome), built as a guesthouse in 1900 by Madho Singh II and now the Textile Gallery, a section of the museum housed within the palace. The Mubarak is a diminutive (by the standards of the royal architecture of Jaipur) marble two-storey building of typical Indo-Saracenic disposition, inspired by the Diwan-i-Khas at Fatehpur Sikri.

The heart of the complex is the seven-tiered Chandra Mahal, or Moon Palace, in which the Chandra Mandir, also housing part of the museum, contains lifesize portraits of the Kachchwahas. The large Sileh Khana, or Armoury on the other side of the peacock courtyard, includes among its exhibits Akbar's general Man Singh's sword, which weighs about five kilograms. The Diwan-i-Khas (Private Audience Hall) contains what are allegedly the largest single pieces of silver in the world — a pair of *gangajalis* made in the palace over a period of two years at the end of the 19th century. The vessels weigh 345 kilograms each and claim to have a capacity of 9,000 litres. Now shaded under delicate cusped arches, the vessels were made for Madho Singh II's visit to England for Edward VII's coronation in 1902; he was the maharaja described by the pioneering British Fabian socialists Sidney and Beatrice Webb in their Indian Journal, written in 1912 but not published until 1987, as 'selfish, sensual and intensely superstitious'. Before he set sail for England the *gangajalis* were filled with water from the sacred Ganges (hence their name) for use in the maharaja's daily prayers and purification rituals while far away from Jaipur.

The palace tells, in pictures, the history of the royal family of Jaipur. The marble elephants carved at the entrance were commissioned by Man Singh II to celebrate the birth of his son, the first male heir born to a ruling maharaja for two generations. So many champagne corks were popped that the boy was nicknamed Bubbles, and the name stuck.

Similarly the art, artefacts, furnishings and manuscripts within the various sections of the palace museum constitute perhaps the most evocative recreation of the opulent lifestyle of the maharajas. Those distant figures languish in the 17th- and 18th-century paintings of the Mughal school — reclining on cushions scattered over the lush fountained terraces of the Jaipur palaces or swinging elegantly on dangling thrones, surrounded by bending fruit trees, spacious pavilions and the violet-blue bloom of the jacaranda, the whiff of frangipani, no doubt, floating through the balmy air. Their descendants are captured in photographs decorously seated on their howdahs atop massive elephants, in procession through the Tripolia Gate surrounded by thousands of adoring subjects. The obsolete howdahs themselves are displayed in the art gallery, elaborately carved and bejewelled. Among the costume collection, look at the heavily

Activity in a barber's shop; a cobbler sits on the roadside under a tattered umbrella

Walls provide free space for the local artist to display his skills or, the hoarding painter to advertise products or services. A brightly coloured billboard displays a selection of local drugs

embroidered thick ankle-length skirts worn by the women of Rajputana. Over the skirts they wear short bodices tied across the back with thin silken cords, an overjacket and a large shawl which doubles up as a veil.

It was in the palace, too, that the whole fairytale was brought to an end. On 30 March 1944, a simple ceremony, attended by eight of the 19 maharajas of the states that used to make up Rajputana, inaugurated the Greater Rajasthan Union.

In 1735, during the reign of Jai Singh II, Govindji, or Krishna in his role as a cowherd, became guardian deity of the rulers of Jaipur. His 18th-century temple, now an inglorious building site, lies in the gardens of Jai Niwas in the direct line of vision of the palace complex.

Nearby, at the open air Jantar Mantar Observatory, the stone instruments have a space-age look, almost like Henry Moore sculptures, and yet they were built in the first half of the 18th century, before Jaipur itself had grown up. The Jantar Mantar is still the largest observatory in India, even though Jai Singh commissioned it over 250 years ago. He was committed to the ambitious task of understanding the universe, and accordingly despatched scholars to the intellectual centres of Renaissance Europe charged with the task of bringing back not military expertise or the spoils of war from neighbouring states, as was the custom of the day, but the latest learned treatises on the configuration of the planets. His first stab at an observatory was in Delhi (also still standing); he went on to build several others, of which this one, at his royal seat of Jaipur, is the biggest and the only one made of stone. Jai Singh went on to write an astronomical tome of his own.

The instruments, restored in 1901, tell the time and perform a range of other functions such as calculating the height and position of celestial bodies, and they consist of huge and dramatic curving sweeps of marble; among them you feel like Gulliver in Brobdingnag. These constructions exert a powerful sense of soaring movement. The cartoonist Nicholas Garland, in his 1983 *Indian Journal*, notes 'a de Chirico-like beauty'. It is an extraordinarily abstract architecture, its staircases, their overlarge steps hollowed by generations of curious observers, ending nowhere — as if they are indeed leading up to the heavenly bodies. Someone should film Jack and the Beanstalk here. The whole observatory is surrounded by a niched wall and a weedy garden, and from the top of the tallest staircases all the landmarks of Jaipur are visible, including the cutout outline of the Hawa Mahal against an azure Rajasthan sky.

Around the corner, near the Tripolia (triple-arched) Gate and the thoroughfare which funnels through it, jammed with bikes and rickshaws, an open urinal is thoughtfully tiled in pink to match the city walls. The thoroughfare leads through to the main drag, and, turning right, the visitor soon arrives at the foot of the Iswari Minar Swarga Sal, the 'minaret piercing heaven'. Look up now and your head spins. Built by Iswari Singh, one of Jai Singh's five offsprings and his rather vapid successor, the Swarga Sal can't help being a landmark, it's so high. It is a bright cream, three-tiered confection shooting skyward and the best vantage point from which to observe it is the roof of the building across the road, reached through an alley of government-owned wholesale shops, above a small gem factory where men sit cross-legged on the floor showering themselves with the fine red sparks of a blowtorch.

Jaipur has other architectural delights. The labyrinthine side-streets of the old city are crammed with *havelis*, merchants' or landowners' houses built around courtyards. Many are festooned with balconies, eaves and porticoes which tangle with a web of electricity cables and feature drying-washing and the odd cat, and squeezed between them a stenographer types or a seller of tiffin tins rattles his wares. Even in the more modest quarters idiosyncratic features lurk among the welter of construction, and certain areas retain the distinctive flavour conferred upon them when the city was founded in the 18th century: the Silvaton ka Mohalla, for example, is the district inhabited by the stone-carvers invited by Jai Singh when Jaipur was built. Other *mohallas* were reserved for different trades, each with its own style, like medieval European guilds. At one time all the houses were painted pink — not to the universal satisfaction of visitors, as is obvious from the different comments. A certain G W Forrest, Director of Records for the Government of India at the turn of the century, noted that the houses 'look well in the bright sunshine, but we miss the gloom and shadow, the mystery and romance of an Oriental city ... it is merely spectacular'. Commenting on Andre Chevrillion's fulsome description of Jaipur as 'India of novels and the opera, fairylike and incredible', Forrest notes sourly, 'The fairyland of the Parisian opera, but not of the Arabian Nights'.

So it is then that one figure presides over Jaipur like a benign deity. Wherever you look in the byzantine old city, the ghostly presence of Jai Singh lingers, the prince who came to the throne of Amber in 1699 when he was 11 years old. As one version of the story goes, when the boy went to Delhi to pay his respects to the Mughal emperor Aurangzeb, the latter was so impressed that he later bestowed upon him the hereditary and oblique title Sawai, which means one-and-a-quarter, in other words, greater than other men. Other accounts have him earning the title on the battlefield while still in his early teens. His father had presided over a revival in the fortunes of the state, which had declined in influence at the Imperial Mughal court just as the stock of neighbouring Jodhpur had risen.

Jai Singh was one of the Kachchwahas, a people who came from near Gwalior to the territory then known as Dhundhar in the 11th century or thereabouts; the land had long been occupied, however, by other tribes. A good deal of Kachchwaha history is shrouded in myth; they claim descent from Kush, the second son of Rama, the protagonist and hero king of the *Ramayana*. In the 16th century the Kachchwaha Rajputs formed an alliance with the Mughals to safeguard their territory. The Rajput states, positioned dangerously close to the Delhi-Agra axis, constituted an omnipresent threat to the Mughals. Jaipur was the first state to accept Akbar's supremacy, and soon only Udaipur held out. That the Rajputs were true allies was symbolised by Akbar's marriage to a Jaipuri princess.

Jai Singh was ousted after Aurangzeb's death for supporting what turned out to be the wrong side in the inevitable war of succession, but along with other Rajput princes he succeeded in reclaiming his territory and his throne. He was a born leader, and something of a Renaissance man. It was a sign of his

The langur monkey, a common sight in and around Jaipur; the sun, symbol of the local dynasty, adorns lampposts in Johari Bazaar

Arched entrances whether leading into palaces, residences or side streets are integral to the architectural landscape of the city. An arched shop-front of a nagra, or indigenous shoe, shop; Girls under the cool colonnaded passage to their school

confidence in Jaipur's military might that he could devote so much of his adult life to intellectual pursuits rather than soldiering, and that he felt sufficiently secure to decamp from the hilltop safety of his court at the famous Amber Fort to the more exposed plain where he built Jaipur. For it was from the overcrowded enclave of Amber that Jai Singh decided, in 1727, to unite Rajputana in a new capital on the dried-up lake bed to the south. It was to be the first planned Rajput city, and although its name has evolved through many metamorphoses, it has always featured with the syllable Jai, which, besides being the founder's own name, means 'victory', and it was in this spirit of triumphant optimism that the pink city came into being.

Although this royal vision could not withstand the forces of history when democracy was to render the princely states obsolete in a new India, still Jai Singh's dream has echoed down the centuries as Jaipur became the administrative and commercial capital of Rajasthan State when the latter was created in 1956. It is a much enlarged state, as Jai Singh's territory constituted but a fraction of modern Rajasthan and was only the fourth largest of the Rajput states. But there was no urban centre to rival Jaipur, which remained independent until it was subsumed within India in 1949.

To design Jaipur, Jai Singh engaged the services of a young Bengali scholar called Vidyadhar Bhattacharaya who had risen to high rank; the city was conceived according to the ancient Hindu architectural treatise, the *Shilpa Shastra*. A simple grid system embraced seven blocks of buildings (some secondary sources claim nine is the magic number, including the two blocks of the palace) divided by wide, tree-lined avenues and a palace and enclosed within a crenellated, seven-gated wall. Although pink sandstone was used for certain buildings, the characteristic pinkness of the whole city was the work of Maharaja Man Singh who renovated Jaipur in the 1870s. The original old city was white.

The pink renovation, in fact, was in honour of a visit by Albert, Prince of Wales. The Rajput princes of Jaipur, who first entered into political negotiations with the British in 1803, initially to form an alliance against the Marathas, were devoted to the British royal family until the end. They were loyal to the British crown during the Mutiny, for which the maharaja was rewarded with a knighthood, among other honours, and when Victoria became Empress of India they were designated feudatories, or vassals.

Jaipur, which was destined to be presided over by a succession of ten maharajas, flourished from the beginning, not least due to the religious tolerance of its ruler, which drew settlers, but also for their active encouragement to merchants and tradesmen. Jai Singh was also a great patron of the arts, and his court attracted a range of painters and other artists, making 18th-century Jaipur one of the most lively cultural centres of the subcontinent. Jai Singh, the great humanist, died in 1743, aged 55.

Jaipur's early history was clouded by the constant threat of the Marathas, and as these latter were gradually worn down by the ever-encroaching British, the power of the maharaja too was eroded. The city, though, continued to flourish, as it still does. M I Road, as Mirza Ismail is known locally, is a thriving commercial centre, and while it may not be pretty, it does reflect the solid manufacturing base of the modern city. From an early stage, residential quarters spilled beyond the confines of the pink walls. Below M I Road the new city peels off into quieter avenues such as Tilak Marg with its pleasant park garden. On this wide and quiet street, lined with bougainvillea-clad villas, they even built the State Bank of Bikaner and Jaipur out of the famous pink stone. Despite this bourgeois affluence, not far off the dispossessed of the city lie on the pavement under makeshift canopies while their children play naked in the gutters. Today Jaipur supports a population of one-and-a-half million.

In the Ram Niwas gardens to the east, at any given time, committed Jaipuris are engaged in the popular Indian pastime of lounging in the grass and concentrating on doing nothing. It is a living park, and men play cricket on the scratchy grass behind the administrative buildings of the museum. It was laid out under the orders of Ram Singh II, though in his day it was larger than the 36 acres it currently occupies. Ram Singh's rule, which began in the mid-19th century, heralded a kind of Renaissance for Jaipur, and he embarked on an ambitious expansion programme. Forrest called Ram Niwas 'one of the finest gardens in India'. Besides the Jaipur Zoo, the Modern Art Gallery, a college and a crocodile breeding farm, Ram Niwas is also the home of the Albert Hall.

It may not resemble London's Albert Hall but it is every bit as grand; ivory coloured with four domes, endless parapets and balustrading, brickwork and *jali*, colonnades and courtyards. It is a multi-layered, complicated and bewitching building much favoured by pigeons whose feathers cover the lawns; frequently taking off together in a huge wave of flapping which momentarily drowns the steady wail of music as a thousand shadows pass over the pale marble.

The architect, Colonel Sir Samuel Swinton Jacob, was an Englishman whom the enthusiastic Ram Singh appointed chief engineer of the state. He went on to work for the Raj administration in Delhi, and his Jaipur creation was allegedly modelled on London's Victoria and Albert Museum; while it is predominantly Indo-Saracenic, notice how it has been touched by the Gothic hand of the Victorians. It was commissioned by Ram Singh to commemorate the visit of Albert, Prince of Wales, in 1876, and the latter laid the foundation stone. He also shot his first tiger while in Jaipur, to everyone's delight, unperturbed by the fact that one of the royal entourage, Major Bradford, a former Resident of Jaipur, had lost an arm to a tiger. Sir J Fayrer, the Prince of Wales's doctor on the trip, wrote an entertaining account of the visit, printed in 1879 for private circulation only. He notes that the streets of Jaipur contained several tigers in cages.   They weren't the only wild animals in town. In *Picturesque India*, published in 1890, W S Caine observed the maharaja's grooms leading black panthers or leopards through the streets...

Inside the Hall the shifting sun strikes the tiles of the cloistered courtyard with moving bars of matt black. Upstairs, above the finger-smeared glass of the dusty cases in the central museum, a crocodile hangs between a bust of Marcus Aurelius and a model of a steam engine. As in every museum, however, it is not these things but a cross-section model of an erect penis which attracts the attention of a lively group of school children from Udaipur.

The painted façade of an old house in Jaipur city. A niche above the doorway contains an image of Ganesha; the elephant-headed god who bestows good fortune

A doorway at Nahargarh Fort, blocked and bolted against intruders. A detail of the old iron lock. Such locks can be found today in bazaars and antique shops

Downstairs a turban map (turbans have been worn in Rajasthan since the second century, and at that time they were not the exclusive province of men) illustrates the seven kinds once worn in the Jaipur district. Alongside are examples of the celebrated Jaipur brasswork, hammered, embossed, engraved, repoussed, perforated and coloured. They include decorative shields depicting scenes from the *Ramayana* and *Mahabharata*, and intricate embossed salvers in an elaborate floral design.

Arriving at the Jai Mahal is quite an event, as one is greeted by a squad of bewhiskered Rajput lookalikes, the tails of their elaborate turbans falling far down their backs. Bougainvillea froths among the terraced Mughal gardens at the rear and two more turbaned characters play music on the lawns against a background of high-domed *chattris* and cupolas with intricate latticework, the familiar blend of Mughal and Rajput. The Jai Mahal was probably developed in the mid-18th century during the reign of Ishwari Singh by his prime minister, Hargovid Natani, and it was called Natani ka Bagh; it later became the property of the state. In the 1860s it was used as the home of the surgeons of the British administration, and later the official residence of the prime minister of Jaipur, which it remained until 1948. It was renamed the Jai Mahal Palace when it was converted into a hotel in 1952.

The Jai Mahal is a sumptuous hotel, but it is the Rambagh Palace which is the abiding icon of modern Jaipur. Again, it is the urban din and hot claustrophobia that stimulate the visitor to appreciate and savour this other Jaipur. Owned by the erstwhile royal family, the building was conceived in 1835 by Ram Singh as a four-roomed garden pavilion for Kesar Badaran, the wetnurse of the prince. Over the course of time it evolved into a hunting lodge, was further moulded into shape by Sir Samuel Swinton Jacob, acquired its own polo field, by the early 20th century was a multi-roomed mansion, and, when Man Singh, the last maharaja, moved in 1925, it was elevated to palace status.

In 1940 Man Singh called in Hammonds of London to do the interiors and Lalique fountains were shipped over from Paris. Gayatri Devi records that when she moved into the Rambagh, her husband bought her the latest model of gramophone, the kind which took several records at once and turned them over. More than 400 servants were employed, including nine cooks (four for English food and five for Indian) and groups of boys whose task was to shoo off pigeons. The governess' dogs drank mineral water which was specially imported from France.

In 1949 the Rambagh was designated the official residence of the Rajpramukh, the Head of State of the new Rajasthan Union and a title conferred (for life) by way of a kind of bungled compensation on the maharaja, who had unceremoniously been put out of business by the relentless march of history. It became a hotel in 1957, much to the horror of the two surviving maharanis who, understandably, were rather fond of it. Gayatri Devi, the younger of the pair, wrote of the loss in her autobiography, 'It seemed like such a concrete symbol of our vanishing way of life'.

The Rambagh, which now has 47 acres of grounds and over a hundred rooms, has many features to cherish. They include splendid examples of the famous Jaipur glazed blue and white pottery tiles; the indoor fountain in the huge sitting room of the Prince's Suite and the pair of gleaming silver herons nearby (the exercise bike in the dressing room adds a modern touch); the painted ceiling in the Suvarna Mahal dining room; the swimming pool, illuminated at night (Nicholas Garland suggested in his book that Hockney should visit it), and the charming stygian gymnasiums. Even though the occasional dance performances among the blazing flowerbeds on the lawns are tailor-made for the tourist, they draw on the city's artistic traditions: with Lucknow, Jaipur is one of the two main centres of the Kathak dance, originally performed only by men (women do dance Kathak now — but they have to dress as men).

In 1956 Man Singh moved out of the huge and costly Rambagh into a much smaller palace only a few minutes away by Bentley. His wife used to sneak back to use the pool, posting a maid outside to fend off hapless guests daring to try to join her. The new palace, which swiftly acquired a pool of its own, was called Raj Mahal, or royal residence. Still owned by the late maharaja's eldest son, it is now also a hotel. The Raj Mahal is not such an aesthetic feast as the Rambagh, but it only has 12 rooms so its appeal lies in its scale. It was built in 1729 by Jai Singh for his maharani, Chandra Kunwar Ranawatji. In 1821 it became the home of the British Resident; the Webbs who were guests of Colonel Showers, the incumbent, in 1912 described it ambiguously as 'somewhat splendidly furnished in quite good taste'. In 1948 it was converted into a guesthouse on the occasion of the marriage of Man Singh's only daughter and eldest child to a maharaja from Gujarat; the event made it into the Guinness Book of Records as the most expensive wedding ever held. In 1956 the princess' father renovated the palace, renamed it and moved in. He lived there until he died. This was where Jackie Kennedy stayed during her celebrated visit to Jaipur.

To the south of both the Rambagh and the Raj Mahal there is another Jaipuri landmark, though of a different kind. The Shri Lakshmi Narayan temple was a devotional aspiration of Shri Braj Mohan Birla and Smt Rukmani Devi Birla; inaugurated in 1985, it is funded by the Hindustan Charitable Trust of the Birla industrial group. This enormous and vaguely sinister construction is an unnatural aspirin-white inside and out with glistening marble floors; even the enormous terrace is free of the merest speck of dust. The contrast with the gloomy pinky-brown stained Moti Doongri Fort directly above and the pale pink concrete buildings of Rajasthan University campus on one side is disconcerting, and the temple exudes a faintly Orwellian chill.

The history of Jaipur reverberates beyond both the city walls and the southern and western urban overspills. Leave through the Jorawar Singh Gate to the north and find Gaitor, the site of the Kachchwaha royal *chhatris* or cenotaphs, overlooked by some of Jaipur's protective forts on the arid and mottled Aravalli slopes. Here pillared tombs of carved white marble (one is partially pink sandstone) stand in a derelict, overgrown and litter bestrewn garden, and pigeons nest among the splendour of the white mausolea. More than half a million people

Latticed windows with their delicate marble filigree create cool havens within forts and palaces. A silver-plated howdah, tarnished and rather sad, lies abandoned in Jaigarh Fort

Details of motifs painted on walls and ceilings. A vase of flowers; dwarpala or doorkeeper and a panel of lotus in bloom

lined the road from the city when the body of the last maharaja was brought to Gaitor to be cremated, many travelling from their outlying villages on foot. The funeral procession, a mile long, included 600 soldiers and was led by elephants, the chief *mahout* carrying a golden rod which, many generations ago, the Mughal emperor had conferred upon the rulers of Amber. As the late maharaja's eldest son lit the pyre, a 19-gun salute was fired.

Despite the hum of the city, faint in the background, the stillness at Gaitor is overpowering. Perhaps nowhere in eastern Rajasthan so clearly evokes the sentiment *sic transit gloria mundi*. Despite the stunning beauty of the burnished white marble, it is a static beauty, and a potent symbol of transience and corruptibility.

Only a short distance away Madho Singh I built a palace called Jal Mahal on Man Sagar lake; he based it on the Jag Mandir and Jas Mandir on Lake Pichola in his hometown of Udaipur. For some years it was used as a lodge for duck-shooting groups, but is now quite derelict and the lake half-empty, not least due to the depredations of the abundant water hyacinth. It is accessible on foot along a ragged causeway overlooking emerald fields sprinkled with orange-clad figures crouching over their crops. 19th-century travellers refer to alligators (they were crocodiles, actually) languishing in the water, but they too have vanished.

The arches around the bottom layer of the building, once used for mooring, are striped with greenish watermarks, and at the top of the weedy steps the Jal Mahal is quite bare and overgrown; the lake bed below is fetid, and only with an effort of the imagination can the building be conjured up in its glory days. It is a place which is far more impressive from afar than close up. From the barren ridge opposite, the Jal Mahal is a romantic vision of symmetrical elegance, each corner punctuated by a semi-octagonal tower topped with a cupola; it appears to be floating serenely on the surface of the water, cut loose from its moorings.

Further along the valley and a long way up, the Jaigarh Fort presides over Amber; it presides, in fact, over all it surveys, which is a good deal. The guidebooks say that it hovers like an eagle, but this is not right; it is much more static, permanent and rooted than this image conveys. The curious thing is that Jaigarh is deserted, compared with the daily crush at Amber, and yet it is of outstanding interest and has a distinctive charm.

Standing at the other end of the Kali Khoh ridge of the Aravalli hills to Nahargarh, the fort, originally tenth century and known as Chilka-Tola, Kite Castle, was rebuilt and renamed by Jai Singh in 1726. The Kachchwaha treasury, containing the spoils of Mughal warring, was allegedly stored here and was guarded by the Mina tribe, the former rulers of Amber who remained loyal to their conquerors. (The Minas are still the largest tribal group in Rajasthan. Their subjection continued long beyond the Rajputs, and the British administration even had them declared criminals.)

The putative wealth of Jaigarh still lures, for in 1976 the government spent a large sum of money draining the tanks, an operation which yielded nothing except frustration. The fort boasts one of the largest cannons in Asia, called the

Jiwan, with a decorated barrel six metres long. It took four elephants to turn it. But it was never used. Behind it grass-green birds hop on the dark pinky-brown crenellated walls which follow the undulations of the hill, redolent of the Great Wall of China or Hadrian's Wall in the north of England.

The closed courtyard of the Jaleb Chowk (sweet market) houses the Armoury. Each cannon made in the Jaigarh foundry has a name, and its record is carefully and lovingly documented as if it were a living thing. In keeping with the conception of the weapon as a work of art, the cannon heads are elaborately carved into tigers with Rajput moustaches. On a flaking wall the trumpet of a *dhonsa*, the musical instrument played in wartime, provides a convenient nesting site for a pair of pigeons. Beside weapons, the display includes 11th-century camel leather oil containers and a 16th-century version consisting of two camel skins around a clay frame. Refreshingly unadorned after the later ornate styles in Jaipur, Jaigarh offers a welcome spontaneity. The yellowing photographs on the wall, above plain medieval copper wine jars, show the last maharaja chatting with General Franco or inspecting the forward front line in Egypt.

Two temples lead off the sweet courtyard: the Shri Rama Hari, founded in 1225 and now with a modern interior, and the Shri Kal Bhairava, set up by Kankal Ji in 1036 to the guardian deity of the fort. The best part of Jaigarh, however, is at the end, once you have walked right through the palace. There, from the 16th-century Vilas Mandir, an open porch affords a dramatic view over the corrugated hillsides, the reservoir, the modern village and the mighty Amber Fort. This vantage point above all others reveals the truth of the cliche that Amber really does appear as if it is growing out of the rock. The Minas called it, 'Queen of the Pass'.

Amber, or Amer, as it was sometimes known, was, for 28 kings over six centuries, the Kachchwaha fortress palace. It was at Amber that the dynasty rose to power and wealth. Protected on all sides by mountains, Amber constituted the perfect sanctuary through the years of lawlessness and political instability.

The Dilaram Gardens (meaning 'bringing restful tranquility to the heart') which cluster at the foot, furnish a resting place for venerable local inhabitants and a home for hundreds of grey monkeys; the monkeys are a menace, but the old men's minds are also much exercised by birds lurking in the trees, and they upbraid them energetically, undeterred by the fact that their efforts have no effect on the birds at all. At the heart of the gardens the Archaeological Museum has a display of eighth-century sculptures from the area, and on the flagstones nearby men use chalk to play the Indian equivalent of noughts and crosses.

The Kachchwahas built a series of forts and temples on the site before the existing structure was begun. Man Singh I began work on the palace in 1592 and Jai Singh I, who ruled from 1621 to 1667, added various buildings and completed Amber. It was greatly influenced by Mughal styles — unsurprisingly, as Man Singh was commander-in-chief of Akbar's army and deeply involved with the Mughal court. Entering through the Jaleb Chowk, the first impression is of more monkeys, mounds of lurid sweets and spices and a good measure of kitsch to feed the tourist maw. Off this courtyard devotions are still made at the small Kali Mata Mandir, also known as the Shri Shila Devi Temple, on the right just

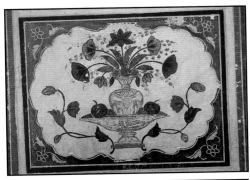

Another rendering of a vase with flowers; a dwarpala or doorkeeper and a decorative panel of stylised flowers and peacocks

Lush terraced gardens surround Sisodia Rani ka Bagh, outside Jaipur, which was built by Jai Singh II for his bride from Udaipur. Women with brightly coloured odhnis work in the fields

before the Singh Pol (Lion Gate). Here a coral image of the goddess trimmed with a marigold garland hangs above the 20th-century silver door, each panel decorated with a painted image and the whole extravagance surrounded by marble inlay. The temple was built in 1604 when Man Singh returned from a military campaign in Bengal, bringing an image of a goddess with him, and it was dedicated to Shila Mata, an incarnation of Kali, the goddess of war. It remained the Jaipur family shrine for generations: if he had been away from the state for any length of time, the last maharaja always went straight to Shila Devi upon his return, and it was his first port of call when he brought his third bride to her new home.

The Singh Pol double gateway leads to a courtyard and the Diwan-i-Am (Public Audience Hall), a stunning Jai Singh addition featuring pink and white double sandstone pillars. From the exquisitely polished cream-and-brown colonnaded terrace overlooking the Maota Lake, its marble floor an interplay of shadows, watch elephants lumbering up the approach road to the Jaleb Chowk, stately and infinitely more dignified than the squirming tourists on their backs.

Proceed through Ganesh Pol or the Elephant Gate, a shimmering and vastly elaborate configuration of aquamarines and chestnut built in about 1640, to the geometric sunken garden of the inner courtyard. The promisingly named Sukh Niwas (Hall of Pleasure) to the right of the garden is irrigated by a water channel, and the design on its stone bed imparts a dancing movement to the flowing water. On the other side of the garden, a palace houses Jai Singh's apartments, and the cusped arches lend a very Moorish hue. The pièce de résistance here are the spectacular jewelled walls of the Jas Mandir (House of Glory) and the dazzling *jali* screens. The Sheesh Mahal (Hall of Mirrors), off the Diwan-i-Khas and allegedly once a bedroom, has no windows. So close the doors and strike a match to see the jewelled ceiling become a glittering sky.

Further into the fort Jai Singh's fairyland gives way to the relative austerity of Man Singh's Palace. He was Emperor Akbar's commander-in-chief in the latter half of the 16th century, and in the blackened older version of the earlier palace the powerful simplicity of the architecture is striking: note, for example, the two simple porches high on the furthest wall. Man Singh ordered 12 suites of rooms for his 12 wives, but elsewhere a pleasing lack of symmetry is evident, accompanied by a faint aroma of decay which clings to the characteristic mottled black- and pink-tinged honey stonework.

The Sisodia Rani ka Bagh — palace and gardens — to the east of Jaipur were built by Jai Singh II for his Udaipur queen, the one he married to cement the revived Rajput alliance. She was a member of the Sisodia clan and she married him on condition that her son would succeed in supercession of his other, elder sons. Her palace, fresh in appearance with its murals of hunting, polo and scenes from Krishna's life, resembles a pagoda, and its manicured lawns are dotted with peacocks. Tranquility is the salient characteristic here. Everyone at Sisodia is affected by languor, as if the place operates as a narcotic. Also to the east, past the pink wedding-cake Hanuman monkey temple, visit the Galita gorge, plunging down from the Aravalli hills and filled with temples and red-bottomed macaque monkeys. Galta is a very holy place, and it is easy to imagine, toiling up the steep steps, the stream of brightly coloured figures going about their devotions on holy days. It is very calm and closed in, background noise supplied by two of the temples which offer live music 24 hours a day, the dominant sound emanating from a concertina.

On the long journey up stop first at the tank, fed by a waterfall from the Gomukh, believed to have curative properties, where women can bathe. This, the first of seven tanks, is decorated in tones of honey, green and brown, and, monkeys slither over the crenellated top of the wall. Behind rises the façade of a building and at the rear of the third 'storey' of this façade is the terrace of the second tank and another cascade of water. This tank is almost 18 metres deep and the men bathe here, next to a diminutive shrine with an attendant priest dispensing sacred water.

Keep climbing, past a white temple and a cluster of buildings abandoned several years ago when the valley was flooded, and suddenly, over the ridge and beyond the sun temple, there is Jaipur. The whole city spreads over the barren soil, over 500 metres above sea level, like a stain. The Aravalli mountains effectively close the pink city off to the north, but here in the south it is wide open to the plains.

In the slums to the south of Jaipur the glorious colours of the poorest inhabitants provide a striking foil for the dull and oppressive monotony of their shacks. Not far off, hideous concrete apartment blocks compete for space with vast new villas, monstrosities of kitsch architecture and new wealth. Sanganer, 16 kilometres from the city and since long a centre of textile block printing, is announced by hillocks of brightly coloured fabric, mopeds heaped with fat skeins and massive square tents of marigold ribbons, like fringed pavilions, hanging by the riverbanks while people work away at sheets of cloth. Away from the noise and movement of the hub of the town, in a quieter quarter life goes on around a complex of intricate Jain temples built by the Digamber sect. The waters of the Aman-i-shah, the river which snakes past the west side of Jaipur, used to fix the colours of the dye used in Sanganer, but chemicals have replaced all that, likewise the ancient vegetable dyes have largely disappeared and, the less labour intensive, screen-printing is popular, squeezing out the *chippa* man who prints with a handblock. Some Sanganer fabrics are dolled up with *kari* printing, a technique which involves embossing with gold or silver.

Papermaking is a spinoff from fabric printing, turning cotton and silk cutoffs into bright pink or yellow sheets, some encrusted with fragments of crushed marigold. Through open doorways try to catch a glimpse of the papermakers, cross-legged, inserting layers of gauze between the filmy sheets. Jaipur blue pottery is also made at Sanganer, with, typically, a cobalt glaze background and hand-painted floral designs in white and copper oxide green.

I have tried to lead you around Jaipur and paint, in words, a thumbnail sketch of a supremely beguiling city. You will see that it has touched many souls. Now you must see for yourself — it will not disappoint you.

A hillside shrine situated in the arid, rocky terrain of the Aravallis. Travellers to Jaipur often encounter sights like this herd of goats meandering along the highway

An artist's impression of Amber, and Amber as it exists today
as seen from Jaigarh Fort.

(opposite) *Elephants with their howdahs full of excited tourists, plod up the
hill to the fortress of Amber.*

(previous page) *Jal Mahal, perfectly proportioned and distinctly palace-like, was actually
built by Madho Singh I (1750-1768) as a lodge for duck-shooting parties.*

During the brief monsoon, the arid landscape and gardens surrounding Maota Lake are transformed. The lush greenery is a total contrast to how the same area looks during the dry season.

(opposite) The sunken garden in the inner courtyard at Amber shows a distinct Mughal influence. Water channels leading to sunken pools with fountains intersect the green areas, where a variety of flowering shrubs bloom. A detail of the geometrically laid out Kesari Kyari (below) or saffron flowerbeds, where each space was filled with the most exotic flowers.

The Sheesh Mahal or Hall of Mirrors is a small, magical room just off the Diwan-i-Khas. The walls and ceilings of the entire chamber are covered with patterns and embellished with countless, tiny mirrors which glimmer under lamp light.

(previous spread) Ganesh Pol, or Elephant Gate, probably the most beautiful gateway in Rajasthan, is covered with mosaics and paintings of Mughal motifs. Delicate lattice screens in marble fill the windows. A fresco of Ganesha, the elephant-headed god of good fortune, can be seen above the main entrance.

A hawker at Jaleb Chowk selling a variety of spicy Indian
snacks. Mounds of peanuts, dried lentils and chickpeas are invitingly piled on
large brass vessels.

A stained glass window of Radha and Krishna.

(opposite) Arches add symmetry to interior spaces. In Amber, the arch has
been widely used as can be seen in the colonnaded hall (above) or to frame the
latticed windows of Jag Mandir Niwas (below).

Nahargarh or Tiger Fort, built by Jai Singh II in 1734, looms above the foliage. This citadel was strategically situated to the northwest, overlooking the city of Jaipur.

The frescoed walls of a chamber within the fort-palace.

(previous page) A panoramic view of Amber valley with a glimpse of Nahargarh Fort perched on a hill top.

Jiwan, believed to be the largest cannon in the world, stands under a protective awning. The six metre long barrel is decorated with elephants, flowers and birds. Despite its impressive size, the cannon was never used because as the notice proudly claims, the rulers' strong defence system deterred enemies from entering the fort.

Garh Ganesh on the way to Nahargarh Fort.

Johari Bazaar is a shopper's paradise. Bales of cotton fabric in bright colours, some unpatterned, some traditionally tied and dyed, are freely available.

Gates are a common sight in Jaipur city. They lead into the City Palace (opposite) where a cyclist swerves to avoid a camel cart. Ajmeri Gate (below) is one of the seven fortified gateways to the city.

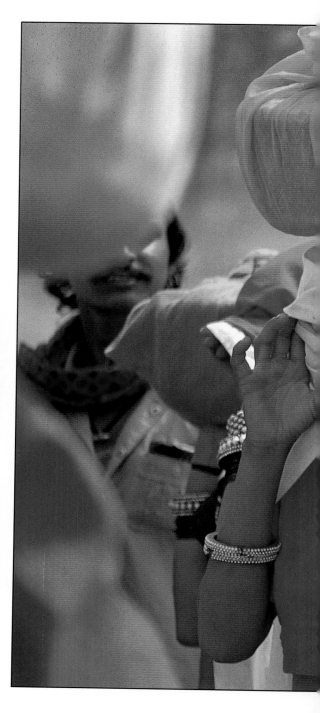

(previous spread) *A large hand-painted hoarding with cutout figures of the protagonists outside the Prem Prakash Cinema House in the walled city. Such hoardings advertising films are part of street scenes all over India.*

The streets of Jaipur are ablaze with colour.
During Holi, the Festival of Colour, gulal or
the powdered colours are heaped on the
roadside drawing customers by the dozens
(top left). Flowers (middle left) are sold
throughout the year as offerings to the gods or
to be strung into garlands. During Diwali, the
Festival of Lights, cheerfully painted toys
made of clay suddenly appear (left). Heavily
veiled women carrying babies with utensils
wrapped in colourful cloth poised on their heads
are a familar sight in the local bazaars (above). A
roadside shop selling cigarettes and paan or
betel leaf (right).

Jaipur's signature building, the Hawa Mahal or Palace of the Winds, was built by Maharaja Pratap Singh in 1799. Located in the centre of town it is a pink sandstone facade, five storeys high but only one room deep. However, when seen from the Samrat Yantra at Jantar Mantar, one gets another completely different view (above).

(previous spread) Hawa Mahal was a discreet vantage point from where the ladies in purdah, peering through the perforated windows, could watch the action below

The gigantic stone instruments of the Jantar Mantar appear like pieces of contemporary sculpture. However, besides telling the time, these complicated astronomical instruments performed a range of other functions like calculating the height and position of celestial bodies. The large circular Ram Yantra and Digamsha Yantra (above) read altitudes and distances in the sky; the Jai Prakash Yantra (right), Jai Singh's invention, told both the time and the sun's path in the heavens; the Samrat Yantra (opposite) is really a giant sundial.

(previous spread) A view of Jai Singh's Observatory with the City Palace in the background. Jai Singh's fascination for science, mathematics and astronomy led him to build massive open-air observatories not only in his captial city but also in Delhi, Mathura, Ujjain and Varanasi.

The City Palace complex, an oasis located in the midst of the bustling old city,
was once the offical residence of the maharaja. Portions of the sprawling area
of palaces connected by courtyards leading into well laid out gardens have been
converted into a museum. The Chandra Mahal or Palace of the Moons (above), in the
centre of the complex, is a seven-tiered structure which was once the royal
apartments. Today it houses part of the museum containing lifesize portraits of
the Kachchwahas. (opposite) Old retainers in an arch set in the Peacock Gate.

(previous spread) The Diwan-i-Khas in the City Palace contains what are
believed to be the largest single pieces of silver in the world. The two urns were
commissioned by Sawai Madho Singh II to contain water from the sacred Ganges
River when he visited England to attend the coronation of Edward VII.

Different views of the City Palace complex. The colonnaded arches of the balcony of what is today the Textile Museum overlooking an inner courtyard. Long corridors stretch along the length of the main palace leading to exquisite little alcoves with delicate marble screens.

Decorative marble inlaid panels are also seen on the walls. Floral motifs delicately etched in marble have been inspired by patterns in the Taj Mahal in Agra.

The painted honeycomb ceilings in the City Palace. Marble images of deities crown symbols of the sun from which the Kachchwahas claim their lineage.

Enormous doors made of bronze lead into the various apartments, like the zenana (above). Some of the doors are engraved with scenes from the life of the young Krishna, the guardian deity of the rulers of Jaipur. In this door (right), one panel shows Krishna in amorous dalliance with Radha, another of him in a playful mood, hiding the gopis' clothes while they bathe in the river.

A detail of the huge silver urn which contained sacred water for the maharaja to cleanse himself while away from Jaipur (left). An interesting arrangement of old rifles adorns a blank wall inside the palace (above).

All kinds of merchandise are available in the numerous bazaars, each of which are indigenous to the Rajasthani way of life. A shop selling saddles and other accessories (above), another selling jootis or the local hand-embroidered leather shoes (right), while a grain merchant chats with his customers outside his shop (below).

(previous spread) A perfume seller with his aromatic wares sits in an alcove in Amber Fort.

A rather decrepit entrance to a stencil shop. Stencils
are used to decorate walls with colourful motifs
or to print signages (above). An array of the local
bhai khatas or accountant books with their distinctive
red bindings (left). Silver ornaments and utensils are
considered status symbols and almost every silversmith
conducts a brisk business as buying continues throughout
the year. Often customers bring old ornaments to sell
or exchange for new ones.

No city is complete without its people. In Jaipur, the old and the young, the traditional and the modern co-exist with ease. Despite the heat, the noise and the bustle, friends can find quiet corners to discuss world or local affairs, or the photographer can set up an improvised studio to catch stray passers-by who may want mementoes of their visit to the pink city.

Over almost all of India, roadside shrines can be found for the devout to worship the deity of their choice. Jaipur is similarly dotted with shrines, some large, some small, some vermilion smeared stones under sacred trees. The bull, Nandi, being worshipped in a Siva temple (top) while (top right) a close-up of Hanumanji, the deity in a small shrine in Cholti Chaupar.

Albert Hall, today the Central Museum, was built to commemorate Albert, the Prince of Wales's visit to Jaipur in 1876. The impressive multi-layered structure, with its many domes, endless parapets and balustrades, colonnades and courtyards, looks as impressive during the day as it does when illuminated at night.

(previous spread) *The Shri Lakshmi Narayan temple, built in the nineteen seventies, is recent introduction to the monuments of the city. Built entirely of white marble, it also promises to be India's first air-conditioned temple.*

The excessive use of red sandstone gave Jaipur the name of Pink City. The Town Hall (above) is today the Legislative Assembly of Rajasthan. A residence in Johari Bazaar (left) in the characteristic style of the city.

Statue Circle where Sawai Jai Singh II stands sentinel over the city he planned and built (above). Ishwar Lath (right) is another major landmark in the city and can been seen from great distances, rising seven storeys high. The local name for this victory tower literally means a dart piercing heaven.

Folk performers, puppets and young girls modestly draped in brightly coloured odhnis are all part of the local colour.

The Rambagh Palace, once the royal residence, today Jaipur's most prestigious landmark. Hotels, especially the super-luxury ones, are the palaces of today where the weary traveller can savour, at a price, the comforts of a bygone age. Balconies overlook the well tended gardens while the Polo Bar (below) has a soothing ambience to enjoy a quiet drink.

Many of Jaipur's palaces and havelis have been converted into hotels. Ramgarh, the family's erstwhile hunting lodge (middle), Raj Mahal, once the Residency of the British Raj (left) and Narain Niwas (top) are all small hotels which cater to a select group of tourists. (opposite) The lounge, inner courtyard and bedroom of Bissau Palace, another hotel privately run by the family who once owned a thikana outside Jaipur State.

Diggi Palace. A brightly painted blue door with floral panels painted on either side leads into a room (below). An inner courtyard (above). The thakurs have converted part of their ancestral home into a hotel, while the gardens teem with polo ponies, buffaloes, cows, geese and dogs.

(opposite) A bejewelled elephant ceremonially clad for a procession.

Pilgrims on their way to Galtaji, the sacred
spring (previous spread). In arid Rajasthan
all sources of water are venerated. Local
women spread their clothes to dry along the
parapets, adding colour to the scene (above).
Water gushes from a cow-shaped spout (right).

(opposite) Jharokas, some painted, some
carved, embellish the buildings at Galtaji.

The royal cenotaphs at Gaitor, just below Nahargarh Fort, are set in beautifully landscaped gardens. Intricately carved pillars, marble domes and platforms were erected over the areas where the maharajas were cremated.

(previous spread) A view of the Chatri of Madho Singh II, a beautifully composed structure in white and pink marble.

Entrance to the Jain temple at Sanganer (opposite). Within, in the inner sanctum, the deities await worship (above) A detail of a carving (left).

Sanganer, the small village outside Jaipur, is a craft village renowned for its handblock printing. Wooden handblocks are carved by hand, dipped in the dye, now mainly chemical, and used to print long lengths of fabric. Large vats contain either dye or water to wash the freshly printed cloth to set the design.

The small jewel-like palace of Samode outside jaipur. Built By Jai Singh's finance minister, the simple exterior belies the wealth of decoration within. The entrance to the palace (above). A view of a mable fountain in one of the inner courtyards (below).

(previous spread) A view of the tiny village of Samode after the monsoon.

A view of the lounge with its frescoed walls and ceiling (above). Another marble fountain (below).

The engraved silver sofa in the lounge, the dining room. Details of a jharoka and fresco.

The charm of Samode lies in its embellishments. It is as if the artists and builder conspired together to make this the most perfect palace in the state. Each portion of the inner surface has been elaborately painted with intricately detailed frescoes. No area is left unadorned. In fact, Samode's beauty is famous worldwide and since its discovery, it has been the location for many films.

Jaipur is famous for its precious and semi-precious stones and its jewellery, especially kundan work. At Gem Palace, the jeweller, Munnu, designs his royal collection (opposite top). The design for an emerald and ruby necklace (left). Peering through the window, a casual passer-by may view the display of necklaces, earrings, bracelets while in the centre is an antique watch in the shape of an umbrella (above). A corner in the shop displays photographs of dignitaries past and present including the present maharaja, Col Bhawani Singh, his wife and daughter, Lord Mountbatten, the last Viceroy, and Pandit Nehru, Independent India's first Prime Minister (right).

(following page) Local bands with their drums, trumpets and banners are often seen during weddings and other times of revelry.